Inca History

500 Interesting Facts About the Incas

Table of Contents

Introduction

Explore one of history's most intriguing empires, the ancient Inca civilization of South America. Discover how this great society rose and fell and influenced the land in ways that can still be felt today. **Many facts will be revealed about the Inca** government and political structure, their religion, festivals, food, clothing choices, and art. Their skills in agriculture and aquaculture helped transform a kingdom into a great empire.

Each chapter will illustrate why the Incas were so successful while also uncovering what led to their ultimate downfall when **they encountered Spanish conquistadors** in the 16th century. **You'll learn about the civil war** between **Huáscar** and **Atahualpa**, Manco Inca Yupanqui, and the rebellion against the Spanish led by **Túpac Amaru**.

Come along on a journey into this ancient civilization where secrets are sure to be discovered!

Emergence of the Inca Civilization
(1200s – 1400s)

The emergence of the Inca civilization in South America is a fascinating topic that has intrigued historians and archaeologists for decades. Examine twenty-five exciting facts about the early Inca way of life, including facts about their military and trade.

1. **The Inca Empire was formed in the 1200s** when different tribes united under a single ruler.

2. **The Inca civilization was located in the Andes Mountains of South America.**

3. **The king, whose title was Sapa Inca,** meaning the great Inca or the only Inca, had a royal palace in Cuzco **(present-day Peru)** made of stone. The palace was decorated with immense quantities of gold, silver, and precious stones.

4. **The Inca people were skilled farmers, builders, and traders.**

5. **The Inca calendar was divided into twelve months based on the solar year.** They also had a calendar based on the position of stars in the night sky. This combination of time reckoning eventually led to inaccuracies, but for the period, it was an amazing achievement.

6. **The Incas built prominent temples to honor gods from different regions of the empire** but also created smaller shrines dedicated to local deities in villages.

7. **They built houses out of stone and mud** and decorated them with colorful fabrics.

8. **Incas believed their terraced pyramid-shaped structures called ushnus** were sacred mountain peaks representing the spiritual power of their civilization.

9. **The Inca used a system of rope bridges to cross rivers** and ravines.

10. **They developed ways to store food by freeze-drying potatoes,** usually the small black potato called papa amarga. This process was called chuño and involved stomping on frozen vegetables to remove moisture.

11. **The Incas used llamas for transport.**

12. **The Incas were very religious and had many gods,** each having special powers over certain elements, such as rivers, mountains, or storms.

13. **The Incas believed in reincarnation and human sacrifice,** though there were different beliefs and practices in parts of the empire.

14. **The Incas were a patriarchal society,** with men holding almost all positions of power.

15. **The coya, the wife of the Sapa Inca, was one of the few women who had real power.** The acllas were priestesses and had influence as well.

16. **They built large fortresses called pucaras** to protect their cities.

17. **Incas were skilled metalworkers** who created tools like axes from bronze or copper alloyed with tin.

18. **Inca artisans made tapestries** and other types of weaving from alpaca wool.

19. **The most important crop of Inca farmers was corn,** which was used in various ways in food and drink.

20. **The Incas believed that the mountains were gods and worshiped them accordingly.**

21. **The Inca had a strong sense of community** and were known for their hospitality.

22. **The Incas had a system of knotted strings called quipus** to record information.

23. **Most cities had plazas for public gatherings and celebrations** where people could come together for worship or entertainment.

24. **The Incas made their capital at Cuzco, Peru,** in the 12th century. The Inca Empire would begin in the 1400s.

25. **The Inca Empire included parts of modern-day Peru, Chile, Ecuador, Bolivia, Argentina, and Colombia.** It covered an area of 400,000 square miles at its peak.

The Reign of Pachacuti Inca Yupanqui
(1438-1471)

Explore Pachacuti Inca Yupanqui's rise to power with these ten interesting facts. Learn why he was one of the most famous Inca rulers of all time!

26. **Pachacuti was the first Inca ruler to rule over more than just Cuzco.** He conquered lands in the Cuzco (Huantanay) Valley and much of modern Peru, northern Chile, and Bolivia.

27. **Pachacuti means "Reverser of the World" or "Earth Shaker."** He became the ninth Sapa Inca and paved the way for the prosperity of the Inca Empire.

28. **Pachacuti rose to power after the Chanca tribe attacked Cuzco,** sparking a conflict. As a young prince, he allegedly summoned the gods to aid the Incas in the fight. They won the war and pushed the Chanca out of Cuzco.

29. **He reconstructed the Temple of Inti in the Coricancha** complex and began work on walls to protect Cuzco.

30. **Pachacuti created a temple in Cuzco so people could worship the creator god named Viracocha.** The Incas worshiped this deity since before the Inca Empire even existed.

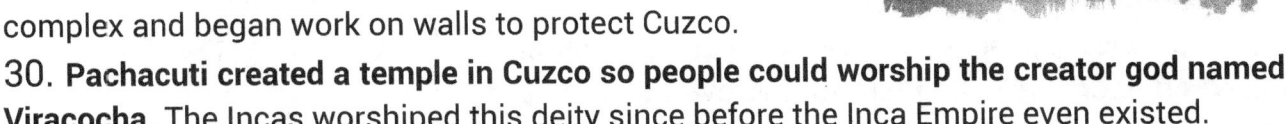

31. **He is famous for transforming the Inca Empire** into an organized state with a strong central government.

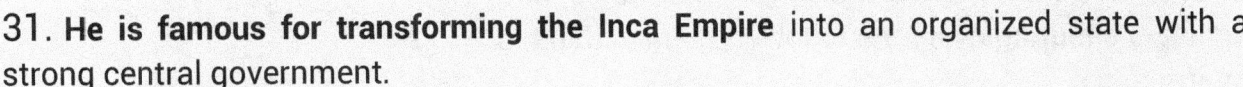

32. **During his rule, Pachacuti built Machu Picchu,** an incredible mountaintop fortress located high in Peru's Andes Mountains.

33. **Pachacuti also built city fortresses like Pisac and Ollantaytambo.** These were important outposts for Inca nobles and agricultural workers.

34. **When he died in 1471 CE, the Incas mourned for a year per his instructions.** They then organized a month-long celebration of their great leader, during which they paraded his possessions around the empire, performed a mock battle in Cuzco, and sacrificed two thousand llamas.

35. **He was later mummified and might have been buried in a shrine called Patallacta** located in Cuzco.

The Reign of Topa Inca Yupanqui
(1471-1493)

Dive into the fascinating history reign of Topa Inca Yupanqui. These ten interesting facts will shed some light on why Topa Inca Yupanqui was a celebrated ruler of the Inca Empire.

36. **Topa Inca Yupanqui was the tenth Sapa Inca of the Inca Empire.** His father was Pachacuti, and his brother was Amaru Inca Yupanqui.

37. **Topa Inca had a son named Huayna Capac,** who inherited the throne.

38. **In 1471, his father abdicated,** with Topa Inca Yupanqui succeeding him.

39. **Topa Inca Yupanqui led successful military campaigns** that greatly expanded Inca territory.

40. **He expanded the empire** into Ecuador and parts of Chile and Argentina.

41. **Topa Inca Yupanqui created a taxation system based on goods,** allowing him to improve agriculture in different areas of the empire.

42. **He passed laws about marriage, inheritance, and language,** ensuring everyone followed them within his empire.

43. **Topa Inca Yupanqui has been compared to Alexander the Great since he essentially continued the expansion program his father started, just as Alexander** did when he inherited the Macedonian throne.

44. **During his reign, he put down an uprising in the Lake Titicaca Basin.** This revolt was likely led by a local leader or tribe.

45. **Topa Inca Yupanqui helped build the Sacsayhuamán fortress** on a high plateau above Cuzco. It had places to store food and clothes.

The Reign of Huayna Capac
(1493-1525)

This chapter will reveal the captivating history of one of the most influential Inca rulers: Huayna Capac. Explore ten facts about his life, accomplishments, and legacy.

46. **When Topa Inca Yupanqui died, Huayna Capac became the eleventh Sapa Inca.**

47. **Although the Incas had a road system in place, Huayna Capac** is known for building two essential roads that helped to improve trade.

48. **Huayna Capac led successful invasions in the north that brought the Inca Empire all the way to the Ancasmayo River,** the modern-day border of Ecuador and Colombia.

49. **Huayna Capac built many new cities and roads** that helped unite distant parts of his kingdom under a single rule for trade purposes and to promote cultural exchange between regions.

50. **Huayna Capac did not name an heir.** Historians believe this could have been due to several factors. He had many sons by different wives, there was political and religious infighting, and **the arrival of the Spanish might have interrupted the process.** Because of the time, place, and changes taking place, he might have named an heir that has been lost to history.

51. **He centralized government bureaucracy, which helped improve economic stability throughout the empire** while ensuring lawfulness through better-organized military forces under a unified command structure.

52. **Huayna Capac was very religious and built many temples** dedicated to the gods of the Inca religion.

53. **He died around 1525 due to a smallpox epidemic** that had spread quickly throughout South America.

54. **Huayna Capac is remembered as one of the greatest Inca rulers.** His legacy lives on through many archaeological sites, monuments, and artifacts that have been preserved to this day.

Civil War between Huáscar and Atahualpa
(1525–1532)

This chapter discusses the civil war between two half-brothers, Huáscar and Atahualpa. Examine ten interesting facts about this conflict, including why it started and how it affected the Inca Empire.

55. **The war began when each brother claimed to be the rightful heir to the throne since their father had died** without naming an official successor.

56. **Huáscar was supported by the nobility. Atahualpa had the support of the majority of the Inca army.**

57. **Many of the battles took place on mountainsides, along rivers, in valleys,** and on the coastlines throughout Peru's highlands.

58. **Dozens of battles were fought in modern-day Peru and Ecuador** as part of this civil war.

59. **Atahualpa governed the Inca army in the northern part of the empire**. He was involved in military campaigns to expand the Inca Empire and include the territory of tribes living in present-day Colombia. Huáscar had his power base in the south.

60. **Atahualpa massacred some of his opponents to strike fear into their hearts.**

61. **By the time the Spanish arrived, Huáscar had been captured by his brother** after having suffered several defeats.

62. **The Spanish forces, who arrived in 1532, proceeded to weaken Atahualpa's rule,** which was already weak from the civil war with his brother Huáscar.

63. **It is likely that thousands died during the Inca Civil War**. It spread disunity at a time when unity was very much needed to fend off the Spanish.

64. **The Inca Civil War has been seen as an important factor in the Inca Empire's downfall** and its subsequent colonization by the Spanish.

65. **The war and its aftermath led to great changes in the region,** as new laws, customs, languages, technologies, and religions spread throughout South America.

The Brief Reign of Atahualpa
(1532-1533)

This chapter will dive into the tumultuous period of Atahualpa's short rule. We'll look at ten fascinating facts about his reign, including his death at the hands of the Spanish.

66. **Atahualpa became Sapa Inca upon his victory in the war with his brother.** But his victory was hollow, as the Spanish began to slowly dominate his kingdom.

67. **Atahualpa was the last effective emperor of the Inca Empire.** Although he officially ruled until he died, his power ended when the Spanish captured him.

68. **Atahualpa was only thirty when he became ruler,** and his rule ended with his death at the hands of the Spanish before or just after he turned thirty-three.

69. **Atahualpa had his brother Huáscar killed while he was in the custody of the Spanish.** Atahualpa did not want Huáscar to escape his confinement and gain control of the empire.

70. **Before the Spanish captured Atahualpa,** he was focused on putting down the remains of Huáscar's forces.

71. **The Spanish plotted an ambush to capture Atahualpa,** hiding men in the town square where Atahualpa agreed to meet them.

72. **Atahualpa rejected the Spanish friar Vincente de Valverde's demands to accept the Christian faith and Spanish sovereignty.** When he refused, he gave the word to Pizarro to capture the Inca king.

73. **The Spaniards executed Atahualpa in 1533.** The death of Atahualpa signaled the end of the Inca Empire and the beginning of Spanish dominance in South America.

74. **After taking power from Atahualpa, Francisco Pizarro declared himself governor of New Castile,** which later became known as Peru.

75. **Following his execution, Atahualpa's remains were buried at Cajamarca,** although some sources say his body was eventually dug up and mummified.

The Spanish Conquest

This chapter explores the Spanish conquest, a monumental period that marked the beginning of European colonization in Peru and forever changed indigenous cultures. We have already touched on how **Francisco Pizarro took over power in the Inca Empire,** so these ten fascinating facts will explore other events of the Spanish conquest and how they changed the region.

76. **Francisco Pizarro led the invasion of what is now Peru in 1532.** He was the second cousin, once removed, of the famous conqueror of Mexico, Hernán Cortés.

77. **It is believed the Spanish were able to overtake the Inca Empire** because of their superior weapons, disunity among the Incas, and the capture of their emperor.

78. **Despite the devastating forces of colonization,** many significant features of Inca culture survived the colonial period and even exist in the present day.

79. **After the conquest, cultural forms, including music and the arts, endured and frequently helped indigenous tribes maintain solidarity** in the face of oppressive socioeconomic conditions.

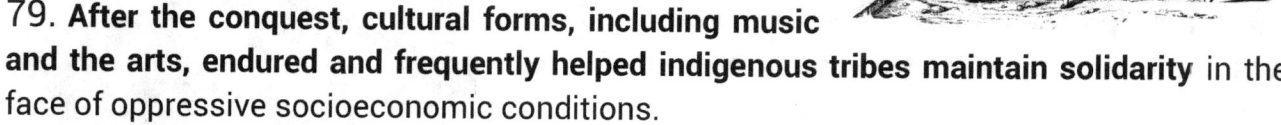

80. **During the Spanish colonial era, art, especially in Cuzco, mixed local symbols and cultural references into religious paintings in the style of the Spanish.** This created a new, hybrid style of religious art.

81. **Indigenous authors who learned to speak and write Spanish sought to reconstruct Inca history** from the perspective of the vanquished in the language of the colonizer.

82. **The Incas were subjected to various atrocities because of colonialism,** which was motivated primarily by a self-interested desire to benefit from economic exploitation.

83. **Franciscan, Dominican, and Jesuit missionaries often allowed aspects of Andean ceremonial rituals to help convert their subjects to Catholicism.**

84. **To create political legitimacy, conquistadors and powerful Spanish families frequently intermarried with the Inca monarchy.** This was called "**mestizaje**," and it is a complex and controversial topic.

85. **With the Spanish capture of the Inca capital of Cuzco in 1533,** Pizarro made Atahualpa's younger brother, Manco Inca, the new emperor of the transitional empire.

Foreign Diseases Spread in the Inca Empire

The devastating effects of disease on the Inca Empire are often overlooked in history, yet it was an integral part of its collapse. These five facts delve into how smallpox and other diseases spread through the Inca population, changing their society forever.

86. **The main disease that affected the Inca Empire was smallpox**. It is a contagious disease caused by a virus and can be deadly if not treated properly.

87. **The Spanish conquistadors were also affected by smallpox,** but they had some immunity from previous exposure to the disease.

88. **The Inca people had no built-up immunity or effective treatment for smallpox,** so many of them suffered and died. It is estimated that around 50 percent of the Incas died of smallpox.

89. **The remaining survivors were left weakened and vulnerable to other diseases,** such as typhus or measles, which further decimated their numbers even more quickly.

90. **The spread of smallpox caused a major disruption in the Inca government,** helping to lead to its eventual collapse shortly after Francisco Pizarro led his forces into Peru.

The Reign of Manco Inca Yupanqui
(1533-1544)

This chapter will unveil the remarkable reign of Manco Inca Yupanqui, a pivotal figure in the history of the Inca Empire. We'll take a look at his legacy by examining ten interesting facts about his life and his courageous fight against Spanish colonization.

91. **Manco Inca was born with the name Manco Capac II, which means "Great Foundation"** in the Inca language of Quechua.

92. **Manco supported Huáscar's claim to power.** When the Spanish captured Atahualpa, Manco initially believed the Spaniards would save Cuzco but realized their goal was the total dominance of the Inca Empire.

93. **Manco Inca was one of Huayna Capac's sons. He became a puppet ruler of the Spanish colonizers** following the murder of Huáscar and the seizure and subsequent garroting of Atahualpa.

94. **The Spaniards openly mistreated Manco Inca while he was in Cuzco,** robbing his home multiple times. The Pizarro brothers (Gonzalo and Juan), who were left in charge of the region, did nothing to stop it and likely encouraged it.

95. **After escaping from Spanish control, Manco Inca led an army of tens of thousands of Inca soldiers against the Spanish conquistadors.**

96. **Manco Inca established his own capital city in the remote region of Vilcabamba,** where he continued to resist the Spanish for several years.

97. **Manco took weapons from the Spanish invaders.** He was preparing his men to use these weapons, adjusting to the changing times of combat, when he was killed in his capital.

98. **In 1544, traitorous Spaniards came to Vilcabamba for safety after killing Francisco Pizarro. They murdered Manco Inca II.**

99. **Manco Inca was known for his bravery and tactics,** but he was also respected for his wisdom and kindness toward his people.

100. **Manco Inca is still celebrated today as a hero of the Inca people,** and his story continues to inspire many indigenous people in South America.

The Reign of Túpac Amaru
(1571-1572)

This chapter will discuss the life and reign of Túpac Amaru, the last ruler of the Neo-Inca Empire. We'll examine ten facts about his resistance to Spanish rule and how that resistance eventually ended.

101. **Túpac Amaru, another son of Manco Inca II,** was the last ruler of the Neo-Inca Empire. **"Neo-Inca" means "new Inca"** and refers to the attempts by the Inca to form a new government after the Spanish invasion.

102. **His name means "Shining Serpent" in Quechua.**

103. **When Francisco de Toledo, the fifth Spanish viceroy of Peru, heard about the chaos after Peru was taken over,** he was determined to put an end to the native people's resistance to Spanish rule and restore Spanish authority with an iron fist.

104. **Though he led an army against the Spanish, Tupac Amaru was not able to win a victory** over the better-equipped and better-organized European enemy.

105. **Túpac Amaru hid in the thick forests east of Vilcabamba,** but Toledo's forces found him and took him away.

106. **Túpac Amaru could have made more progress when escaping,** but his wife was expecting a child, which slowed him down.

107. **Túpac Amaru was publicly executed in 1572 as a symbol of Spain's victory** over him and the Incas.

108. **Many Catholic missionaries believed Túpac Amaru had done no wrong and wanted him to be tried in Spain.**

109. **The Spanish wanted to make an example of Tupac Amaru to discourage further Inca uprisings,** so they hung him. Some sources say thousands of people witnessed his death.

110. **Túpac Amaru was known as a brave warrior** who fought with courage against Spanish forces determined to conquer his people's way of life and resources.

The End of the Inca Resistance and Cultural Change in Peru
(1572-1780)

For centuries, the Inca civilization dominated the landscape of Peru. However, this changed in 1572 when the Neo-Inca Empire fell. **The Inca culture evolved,** featuring a mixture of Inca and Spanish customs, beliefs, and language. Let's look at ten facts about what happened after the Inca resistance ended.

111. **Large-scale Inca resistance to the Spanish ended in 1572 when their leader, Túpac Amaru, was captured** and killed by the Spanish.

112. **The end of the Inca resistance marked a fundamental shift from traditional and indigenous ways of life to a more European society**. However, for many people in the Spanish colony, especially at its beginning, this was not a welcome change.

113. **The Spanish brought new technology and cultural aspects** that had not been seen before in South America.

114. **When the Europeans arrived, they introduced horses, which made it easier to travel through otherwise impassable terrain,** allowing them to conquer more quickly than ever before.

115. **Christianity became a dominant force, replacing many traditional beliefs** held by indigenous groups prior to colonization.

116. **The Spanish established a system of forced labor** that required indigenous people to provide unpaid labor on Spanish-owned estates or in mines.

117. **In 1780, an uprising led by Túpac Amaru II, the son of a Spanish mother and Inca father, a**ttempted to overthrow Spanish rule but ultimately failed. However, this event served as a pivotal moment in Peruvian resistance, setting the stage for the eventual achievement of independence from Spain more than fifty years later.

118. **New foods were introduced to the Spanish,** such as tomatoes, peppers, and chocolate. These foods were eventually brought to Europe.

119. **This period also saw changes in architecture, with churches having Spanish-style facades** while still incorporating typical indigenous features.

120. **By the early 19th century, Peru had developed a distinctive identity** by combining both European and indigenous elements.

Inca Rebellion
(1780-1783)

This chapter delves into the fascinating story of the Inca Rebellion. We'll explore ten interesting facts about the brave leaders of the rebellion, their tactics, and the lasting effects of this tumultuous period in history.

121. **Túpac Amaru II, also known as José Gabriel Condorcanqui, was born in the Tinta** region of Peru. He led the rebellion until his death in 1781.

122. **The Inca Rebellion was a revolt of indigenous people against the Spanish** in South America that lasted between 1780 and 1783.

123. **The Incas under Túpac Amaru II won a major victory at the Battle of Sangarará** on November 18th, 1780. This victory gave the rebels control of the city of Cuzco for a short time.

124. **Tens of thousands of native warriors joined the rebellion,** which spread quickly through Andean regions.

125. **Women were important leaders in the movement. Micaela Bastidas** helped lead troops into battle alongside her husband, Túpac Amaru II.

126. **The rebels used guerrilla tactics to fight off larger numbers of better-equipped Spanish forces** for months on end until they were eventually defeated in early 1782, although pockets of fighting continued until 1783.

127. **The revolt caused economic disruption, leading to food shortages, famine, and disease** among both native and colonial populations.

128. **The famous rapper Tupac was named after Túpac Amaru II** since his mother wanted him to be named after an indigenous revolutionary leader.

129. **Túpac Amaru II was captured by Inca royalists who supported Spain during a battle in 1781** and was sentenced to death by the Spanish.

130. **The Inca Rebellion was dealt a massive blow when the Spanish executed Túpac Amaru II, his wife, and his children** in May 1781. He was supposed to be quartered (dismembered), but the horses failed to rip his limbs off, so he was beheaded instead.

Incas Religion and Spirituality

Delve into the captivating world of Inca spirituality. We'll reveal thirty-five fascinating facts about their religion, including their priests and ceremonies. **Most people know about the Inca because of their military** might; now, it is time to learn why they should be known for their religion!

131. **The Incas believed in many gods and goddesses** that controlled the natural elements like the mountains, lakes, rivers, sun, and moon.

132. **Their primary god was Inti (the sun god),** who the Incas believed gave them life and energy.

133. **Priests were highly respected members of society because they communicated with the gods on behalf of the people.** They asked for protection or favors from the gods, and great care was taken when performing ceremonies or sacrifices at the temples.

134. **The Incas practiced a form of ancestor worship.** They believed their ancestors had the power to influence the future.

135. **In Cuzco, the high priest was called the uma uillaca.** He was at the top of the chain of priests. The hatun uillaca, who acted like a bishop, was right below the high priest. The yana uillaca, or ordinary priest, stood below him.

136. **The Incas believed that drinking tea made from coca, the main ingredient of cocaine, would give them spiritual powers.** This tea was often used in religious ceremonies or consumed by shamans before performing rituals.

137. **Shamans were healers who communicated with gods through visions,** allowing them to diagnose illnesses or provide guidance on important matters such as war.

138. **Music played an essential role in Inca spirituality.** Instruments like panpipes were used during rituals, and songs were sung to honor different deities.

139. Spiritual beliefs also had a practical side. For instance, rites of passage into adulthood included long treks up mountains where one could commune more closely with the gods. **These journeys weren't only about worship;** they were also about gaining strength and wisdom from nature.

140. The Incas believed that some places had a special connection to the gods and held miraculous powers. These places were called huacas, and they played an important role in society.

141. The bodies of many sacrificial victims were taken to high altitudes where the cold, dry air would better preserve their bodies.

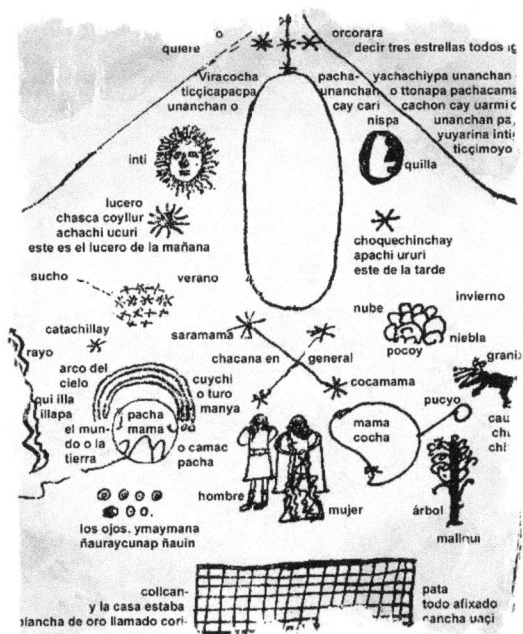

142. One of the most famous Inca mummies is known as the "Lady of the Ampato" or "Juanita." She was discovered in 1995 on the summit of the Ampato volcano in southern Peru. **Juanita is believed to have been a young girl,** around twelve to fourteen years old, who was chosen as an offering to the gods. Her well-preserved mummy provided valuable insights into Inca mummification practices and rituals.

143. Regions of the Inca Empire had a unique system of sacrifice known as capacocha, where children from noble families were selected to be sacrificed and mummified in a ceremony meant to ensure good harvests and protect the empire from harm.

144. Mummification was part of elaborate funerary rituals that emphasized the importance of the deceased's role in the community and their connection to the spiritual realm.

145. The Incas believed that their ancestors' spirits could come back from the afterlife to communicate with them through dreams. These messages were taken seriously as guidance on how best to live life.

146. **Peyote cactus was used during religious ceremonies due to its hallucinogenic properties,** which allowed shamans access to spiritual realms. They also drank chicha, a brew made from other hallucinogenic plants. This practice is still seen today among some indigenous communities.

147. **The Inca god of the underworld was Supay.** He was a powerful god who was feared by the Inca people. **Supay was depicted as a giant serpent with a human face.** He was associated with death, darkness, and evil.

148. **Supay was also associated with earthquakes.** The Inca believed that Supay caused earthquakes when he was angry.

149. **The Incas would often make offerings to Supay in an attempt to appease him and prevent earthquakes.** The entire western region of South America is particularly prone to earthquakes, which likely meant that Supay played a huge role in the lives of the Inca.

150. **Inca mythology includes stories about powerful figures like Viracocha, who created humans out of clay, and Pachamama, the "Earth Mother" goddess.**

151. **They believed in an afterlife and mummified their dead** rulers to help them reach this place.

152. **The Incas buried food, tools, and other items with the dead** so they had items when they arrived in the afterlife.

153. **In ancient times, it was thought that certain mountains were so sacred they could not be climbed.** These sites still exist today and are considered off-limits to people.

154. **Masks made from gold or other materials were used during religious ceremonies.** Each mask had a special meaning, depending on which god it represented.

155. **Shamans often wore masks because they were thought to help them communicate with spirits more easily.**

156. **The Incas believed the world was divided into three parts: hanaq pacha** (the world above), **kay pacha** (this world), and **ukhu pacha** (the world below).

157. **Miraculous healings were thought to be possible through spiritual intervention.** For example, if a person was sick and believed their illness came from an evil spirit, shamans would perform rituals that expelled the bad energy.

158. **Pachamama, or Mother Earth, was associated with agriculture and the earth** and was said to make the fields productive. She was especially influential in the highlands, where agriculture was essential.

159. **It was believed that certain places held powerful energies.** These sites are still considered sacred by many today, such as Machu Picchu in Peru.

160. **The Incas believed in a cosmic order dictated by their gods,** including concepts like the balance between opposing forces and reciprocity (giving back what one has received).

161. **The idea of reincarnation was also accepted by the Incas.** It was thought that after a person died, their spirit could enter another body to continue its journey through life.

162. **Viracocha was the creator of humanity at Tiwanaku in Bolivia or the Islands of the Sun in Lake Titicaca,** which straddles the boundary between Peru and Bolivia. Both locations became important pilgrimage destinations for the Incas.

163. **The Incas believed in a cyclical view of time,** with the world ending and being reborn every five hundred years. **This was called** *pachakuti,* which means "world turnover" or "world reversal" in Quechua.

164. **The Incas believed that the world would end in a series of natural disasters,** such as earthquakes, floods, and droughts. They also believed that the sun would go out and that the stars would fall from the sky.

165. **After the world ended, the Incas believed that it would be reborn in a new form.** The new world would be a paradise with no hunger, disease, or death.

Death and Burial Customs of the Inca

This section will discuss the customs, rituals, and practices associated with death and burial among the Inca from 1200 to 1532. Let's dive into twenty interesting facts about how the Inca honored their dead.

166. **Death was an important part of life for the Inca,** and they had very specific customs surrounding it.

167. **When an important leader died, their body was mummified** and entombed in a special chamber made of stone blocks called a huaca.

168. **After death, many important Incas were buried in elaborate tombs high up on mountainsides** so that their spirits could ascend closer to the gods who lived above the clouds.

169. **Family members would often stay near burial sites for several days** afterward as part of mourning rituals for those who had passed away.

170. **Death in the Inca culture involved two stages.** The first stage was *wañuq*, in which the person who died entered the realm of the dead. After *wañuq*, the body became an *aya*, which means dead body. The spiritual body had separated from the physical body.

171. **In the Inca Empire, certain burial sites belonged to specific families or clans,** most of whom could trace their ancestors back many generations.

172. **Many of these tombs were decorated with colorful murals and sculptures** that helped tell stories about the family's past.

173. **Some graves even contained miniature replicas of houses,** symbolizing a place for spirits to rest after death.

174. **It was a common practice among some cultures to bury their dead** facing east so they could look out over their kingdom while waiting to ascend to the heavens.

175. **The curacas, or regional rulers, were respected in a similar way to royalty.** To help the curacas get ready for the afterlife, they would be mummified and put in a special place that would be filled with different items.

176. **Local people would sacrifice llamas and guinea pigs as part of the ritual** for the curacas and leave fine textiles, ceramics, and chicha at the gravesite.

177. **Mourners often sang songs during funeral processions,** which helped them honor those who had passed away.

178. **Some tribes in the Inca Empire believed that placing rocks on top of graves** ensured protection against evil spirits entering their world after death.

179. **In parts of Peru where the soil wasn't suitable enough to bury people,** families sometimes cremated their dead.

180. **After a body was cremated, the ashes were often placed in urns and buried underground** or scattered around important areas to the tribe, such as rivers, lakes, and sacred places.

181. **It was also a common practice to bury items that had been used by the deceased** while they were alive, such as tools or weapons they had used for work or hunting.

182. **The Incas dressed the emperor's mummified body in a fine *uncu* (tunic), sandals, headdress, jewels, and earspools,** just as he would have donned in life. He was then covered in five to six layers of the finest cumbi textiles (the finest cloth woven from vicuna fur and typically intertwined with silver, gold, feathers, and Spondylus shells).

183. **Some tombs even included mummies of llamas, alpacas, and other animals.** The Incas believed these creatures would help guide their owners safely into the afterlife.

184. **The Inca people often built monuments at gravesites,** including statues of deities associated with death and burial rituals.

185. **For a long time, it was believed that some mummies had been buried alive,** but this is not true.

Human Sacrifice in the Inca Empire

At certain times and under certain conditions, **the Inca, like other pre-Columbian cultures in South and Central America, practiced human sacrifice.** One of the unique things about the Inca was that children were often the victims of these rituals. Here are ten things we know about Inca human sacrifices.

186. **Human sacrifice held religious significance in the Inca culture.** It was believed to appease deities and ensure the well-being of the empire.

187. **Human sacrifices could die by strangulation,** bludgeoning, exposure to cold, or another method.

188. **Each method of death had a distinct purpose and symbolism.**

189. **Child sacrifices (*capacocha*) were performed.** Children were selected for their perceived purity and innocence.

190. **Child sacrifices were typically between the ages of four and fourteen.** They were chosen based on physical attributes, lineage, and other factors.

191. **Sacrificial victims, including children, were treated with respect** and adorned with fine clothing and jewelry before the ritual.

192. **Many child sacrifices took place at locations like mountain peaks or lakes** because they were considered sacred.

193. **Valuable offerings, such as textiles, ceramics, food, and figurines, were placed alongside the victims** as offerings to the gods.

194. **Human sacrifice was linked to the social hierarchy and power dynamics,** with rulers and elites often conducting and benefiting from these rituals.

195. **The practice of human sacrifice, especially child sacrifice, diminished with the arrival of Spanish** conquistadors, who sought to suppress these rituals.

Festivals of the Incas

The Inca civilization held numerous festivals yearly. In this chapter, we will unveil thirty interesting facts about Inca festivals, including the activities they did during them and why they were celebrating in the first place.

196. **The Incas held festivals to celebrate special occasions,** such as harvests, the solstices, and victories in battle.

197. **Festivals often involved dancing, music, and feasting** for hours or days on end.

198. **During some festivals, there would be competitions like running races or ball game tournaments** between villages for prizes, such as food or clothing.

199. **Many festivals included colorful costumes with feathers, jewelry, and headdresses.** Most costumes were made out of alpaca or llama fur.

200. **One of the most important festivals was called Inti Raymi,** which celebrated the winter solstice and the sun god every June 24ᵗʰ. The celebration lasted nine days! Remember, places south of the equator celebrate their winter in the

middle of the year, while those north of the equator are enjoying summer.

201. **During Inti Raymi, a llama would be sacrificed to thank Inti** for all the blessings he had bestowed upon them during the year.

202. **Some festivals included dramatic plays, with actors dressing up as deities and acting out stories** about the creation of the universe.

203. **The Incas would wear large golden masks during the festivals** to represent their gods.

204. **The summer solstice was called Capac Raymi** and was celebrated on December 21ˢᵗ.

205. **One month after the summer solstice, the Capac Raymi Camay Quilla festival,** meaning **"Festival of the Moon,"** was held.

206. **The Incas also celebrated their victories in battle** with feasting and dancing.

207. **The Incas believed their gods would be pleased by the sound of drums, flutes, whistles, conch shells, and chirping birds.**

208. **Another important festival was called the Yawar** (or "Blood") Festival. It was a ritualistic celebration that involved the release and occasional sacrifice of captive birds.

209. **The Yawar Festival was held to honor the mountain gods** and ensure the well-being of the community. It often took place in September.

210. **The Aymoray (Hatun Cuzqui) festival, which means "excellent cultivation,"** was held in May.

211. **During Aymoray, there was a ritual harvest of sacred maize fields,** which was followed by dancing and singing, with the people asking the gods to bless them with enough grain until the next harvest.

212. **There was usually some type of ceremony dedicated to a deity every month.** It is estimated that there were over forty festivals throughout the Inca calendar year.

213. **During an event called Sapa Inca Raymi (or Royal Festival),** people feasted for nine days straight when called by the Sapa Inca. It was often called in times of triumph or celebration, such as naming a new ruler.

214. **The Royal Festival often involved over ten thousand participants,** including priests, warriors, and royalty dressed up in elaborate costumes.

215. **A variety of dances were performed during festivals, such as the Qhapaq Chunchu.** This was a dance associated with the Inca nobility.

216. **Dancers wore elaborate costumes and performed intricate footwork** and hand movements.

217. **Food is an important part of any festival!** Popular dishes included guinea pigs, potatoes, maize, and fruit like papayas and avocados.

218. **During some religious ceremonies, priests would lead people in prayer** while wearing colorful clothing made from feathers and llama fur.

219. **For many festivals, musicians played drums, flutes, and panpipes** to create beautiful melodies that echoed through the valleys.

220. **Other forms of entertainment, such as juggling or acrobatics,** were popular during celebrations too.

221. **Wifala was a dance performed during Inti Raymi** (Festival of the Sun) and other important festivities. It involved dancers forming pairs and moving in intricate patterns while holding scarves or pieces of fabric. The dance symbolized unity and the balance between different elements of the cosmos.

222. **During some festivals, young men would compete against each other in races** or wrestling matches for prizes like jewelry or weapons made from gold or silver.

223. **Huayno is a traditional Andean dance and music style that predates the Inca Empire but continued to be practiced during it.** The dance involves rhythmic footwork and intricate hand movements. Huayno dances often depict scenes from daily life, nature, and the surrounding environment.

224. **The Incas believed it was imperative to live harmoniously with nature,** so they incorporated elements from nature into many rituals and festivals.

225. **The Incas also believed in the power of words,** so they often chanted special prayers during festivals to bring good luck and protection.

Government and Political Structure of the Incas

Analyze **the advanced government of the Inca Empire** in this chapter as we uncover twenty-five intriguing facts about their political structure. Explore how the Inca ruled and how they kept their empire running smoothly.

226. **The Incas were the last great indigenous empire in South America.** The historical record shows organized governments in South America going back to the Chavin culture (c. 900–200 BCE)

227. **The Sapa Inca,** in some ways, was considered the only one with real power in the Inca Empire. Everyone else was a subject.

228. **The Sapa Inca was believed to be descended from Inti, the Inca sun god,** which meant he had divine and political powers.

229. **The Sapa Inca surrounded himself with advisors** who helped him with decisions related to politics and war.

230. **The capital city of the Inca Empire was Cuzco,** located in modern-day Peru. Many essential buildings stood there, including temples dedicated to gods like Viracocha (the creator), Inti (the sun god), or Pachamama (Mother Earth).

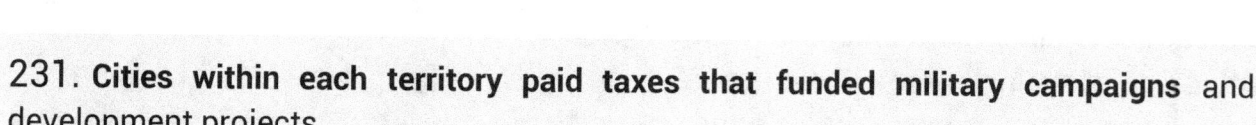

231. **Cities within each territory paid taxes that funded military campaigns** and development projects.

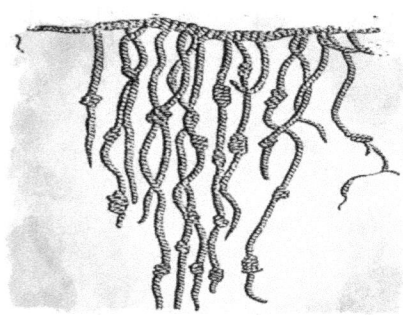

232. **Record-keeping was done through a series of knotted strings called quipu,** which enabled the government to keep track of taxes, tribute, and other important information about its citizens.

233. **The Inca Empire practiced a form of socialism where everyone worked for the common good** but kept some personal property rights.

234. **All land ultimately belonged to the Sapa Inca, who could redistribute it at any time.**

235. **If people disobeyed the Sapa Inca**, they could be put to death.

236. **Social classes were rigidly defined within the government structure.** The nobility and priests were on top, followed by artisans, then peasants at the bottom.

237. **The Incas had a very sophisticated system of justice and laws,** with courts of law to settle disputes between citizens or members of different social classes.

238. **Taxation was done in labor rather than money.** Everyone was required to pay tribute through their work on public projects, such as building roads, bridges, and agricultural terraces.

239. **The Inca religion heavily influenced all aspects of politics.** Religious ceremonies were held for significant decisions made by the Sapa Inca or his advisors. Most historians consider the Inca government to be a type of theocracy.

240. **A complex bureaucracy ran the government, including quipucamayocs** (administrators), **yanaconas** (civil servants), and **curacas** (local governors).

241. **The Inca Empire used various methods to maintain control over its vast territories.** For instance, the Sapa Inca sent out spies to keep tabs on his governors. He also used armies and built fortifications.

242. **The Incas believed in a concept called ayni,** which is the idea of mutual responsibility between citizens to ensure that everyone has enough food, shelter, and clothing.

243. **Each province was divided into smaller units called ayllus,** which were led by a chief called the curaca.

244. **The curacas governed villages according to customary laws set by tribal chieftains.** They also sought guidance from higher levels of authority, like regional governors and even the Sapa Inca himself.

245. **The Inca government was somewhat decentralized, with many regional rulers** who all answered directly to the Sapa Inca or his personal representatives. This allowed them to respond quickly when threats arose from outside enemies.

246. **The Incas sometimes used local religious leaders as intermediaries for dealing with issues** at the local level instead of relying only on the imperial bureaucracy.

247. **Governing an empire of this size required a reliable communication system.** The Incas used a network of runners (known as chasquis) who could travel over three thousand miles in a few weeks. They would hand messages to each other as they traveled from one region to another.

248. **The chasquis were not only runners but also spies.** They reported on any suspicious activity and potential outside threats to the empire.

249. **Community leaders, chiefs, and other respected members of the empire** helped to enforce the laws.

250. **The Inca Empire promoted peace,** but if someone broke the law, their punishment was often harsh.

Food and Cuisine of the Incas

Most people know that the Incas were one of the largest empires in pre-Columbian America. But how much do you know about the food they ate? **Discover thirty interesting facts about their meals;** you might be shocked to learn what some of their most common foods are!

251. **The Incas often ate corn, potatoes, quinoa, seafood, guinea pigs, and llama meat.**

252. **They grew crops on terraces on the sides of mountains** for easy access to water from rivers or springs.

253. **They used condiments like chili peppers and aji** (a type of pepper) to add flavor to their dishes.

254. **Quinoa was considered sacred by the Incas because it provided them with important vitamins and minerals** that were necessary for good health.

255. **Potatoes were one of the most popular vegetables eaten by the Incas.** Potatoes could be stored easily in underground storage rooms called colcas.

256. *Cuy* **(guinea pig) is still served in Peru** as part of traditional meals.

257. **Chicha de jora is a fermented drink made of maize.** During the Inca Empire, it was drunk on special occasions, such as religious ceremonies or festivals.

258. **Locro is a soup-like dish with cheese, potatoes, chili peppers, and onions.**

259. **The Incas believed food was sacred and connected to their gods,** so they had special rituals before eating it.

260. **They ate two times per day on average:** a large midday meal and a lighter dinner or evening snack.

261. **Maize was one of the main staple crops for the Incas.** It was prepared in many ways, such as being boiled, roasted, or made into dough.

262. **The Inca consumed various kinds of edible insects,** which are a good source of protein.

263. **Pachamanca was a dish cooked with hot stones placed inside an oven dug into the ground** and filled with meats, vegetables, and potatoes.

264. **The Incas ate a lot of seafood,** such as fish, mussels, and shellfish.

265. **They used woven straw baskets to store grains and other dried foods.** By keeping food away from moisture, the Incas could enjoy fresh food for longer periods.

266. **The Incas cooked with wood-fire stoves called huatias,** which had vents to regulate the heat.

267. **A popular dish during festivals was tamales made from maize mixed with lard or fat,** chili peppers, onions, and cheese.

268. **The Incas often ate charqui** (dried llama meat).

269. **Incas usually ate on the floor** and did not use a table.

270. **Chicha de molle is a traditional drink made from the red berries** of the molle tree.

271. **Ajiaco is a stew with potatoes, chili peppers, cheese,** and other ingredients like corn or beans.

272. **Ceviche is still eaten in Peru as part of traditional meals.** It's made by curing fish in lime juice mixed with onion, chili pepper, garlic, and herbs.

273. **Potatoes also could be desserts, such as picarones** (deep-fried doughnuts).

274. **Soups played an important role in their cuisine. Locro de zapallo** (pumpkin soup) was made of squash puree blended with potatoes, corn kernels, and herbs.

275. **Quinoa dishes were flavored using spices such as huacatay** (black mint), chili pepper paste, and oregano leaves.

276. **Chuño blanco was a type of freeze-dried potato** that was used to make dishes like soups and stews. It is still eaten today!

277. **The Incas enjoyed various fruits,** such as papaya, guava, passion fruit, and cherimoya.

278. **A popular dish served during festivals was chiriuchu,** which was made from roasted vegetables, chili peppers, and potatoes.

279. **Popular snacks included dried corn kernels called mote or popped quinoa,** which were often sweetened with honey or sugarcane juice.

280. **Incas had a dish called maiz tostado,** which involved roasting corn kernels over an open flame and then pounding them into flour for making tortillas or other dishes.

Clothing of the Incas

The clothing of the Incas is just as interesting as their food. We will divulge thirty interesting facts about the way their clothing was made, as well as common styles.

281. **The Incas used natural materials, such as cotton, llama wool, and alpaca fibers,** to make their clothing.

282. **Clothing for the royal family of the Incas was made from delicate fabrics dyed with bright colors** or decorated with feathers or gold adornments.

283. **Commoners typically had simpler garments, including tunics** (long shirts) made from cotton or wool that could be dyed differently depending on one's status within society. Red was for warriors, and yellow was for priests.

284. **As a form of identification, each class had its own distinct style, which included different hats depending on one's social status.** Royalty could be identified by the more elaborate headgear they wore.

285. **Clothing styles were designed to keep people warm during cold mountain winters** while protecting them from harsh sunlight found in higher altitudes during summer. Many clothing pieces featured long sleeves and high necklines for this reason.

286. **Women usually draped themselves in a wrap-like skirt called an anaku.** This skirt reached to their ankles.

287. **Men wore knee-length trousers and a long tunic with sleeves down to their elbows,** usually made from wool or alpaca fibers.

288. **Footwear for both men and women consisted of sandals made from leather** straps or cloth bands that were adjustable at the ankle.

289. **Nobility often had clothing decorated with precious metals, such as gold and silver.** Their clothing might even have gold and silver thread embroidery in intricate patterns.

290. **In addition to traditional garments, Incas also used various decorative items** like necklaces or pendants worn around their necks, which could be adorned with feathers, stones, and shells.

291. **Textiles were considered very valuable by the Inca people.** They would use textiles as currency when trading goods among one another instead of using coins or other forms of money.

292. **The most common headgear was called a chullo—a hat with ear flaps** designed to protect against the cold weather.

293. **Incas used a traditional form of weaving called a backstrap** loom to create their fabrics.

294. **Women often wore long robes with a large belt around their waist.** Their clothing was usually made from wool or cotton.

295. **Inca footwear was called usutas.** Usutas were sandals that were made from a single piece of leather or cloth.

296. **Most Inca clothing was handwoven on a loom and decorated** with bright colors or intricate designs. This skill was passed down from generation to generation.

297. **The Incas used buttons made from clay** that were then attached with strings or threads.

298. **Royal women wore elaborate headdresses that included feathers, gold tassels, beads,** and pieces of cloth draped across their shoulders.

299. **Inca kings often wore large feathered robes.** These robes represented power and authority.

300. **The Incas wore ponchos.** A poncho consisted of a single rectangular piece of cloth that was worn either around the waist or shoulders like a cape. **Ponchos usually featured intricate designs embroidered** onto their edges.

301. **Clothes had specific purposes according to gender.** Men's clothes were generally for hunting and protection, while **women's garments generally served a decorative purpose** that showed off their social position or beauty through intricate designs and embroidery work.

302. **The Incas used dyes from plants, animals, and minerals to create bright colors** when dying their fabrics.

303. **Incas used natural dyes from things like cochineal bugs or mosses** grown locally near Cuzco (the capital city).

304. **The most prized feathers in Inca society were those of the quetzal bird.** The quetzal is a brightly colored bird that is native to Central and South America. It has a long, green tail, and its tail feathers were considered to be very sacred by the Incas.

305. **Incas often wore layers to protect against the cold climate i**n the Andes Mountains.

306. **Shawls were commonly used to keep warm** and could be made from various materials, including cotton and alpaca and llama wool.

307. **The Incas believed certain colors had magical properties,** which was something they kept in mind when dying clothing.

308. **Tassels were popular decorative pieces** and could be seen dangling from clothing or jewelry as adornments.

309. **Fabrics were often decorated with intricate geometric patterns, animal figures, and symbols** to represent different aspects of their culture.

310. **Young girls wore colorful ribbons in their hair,** which was considered a sign of beauty. These hair decorations could range from simple ties made of wool fabric to more elaborate designs featuring gold beads.

Art and Stories of the Incas

This chapter details twenty-five incredible facts about Inca artwork and stories. We talk about **their intricate textiles** and **beautiful sculptures**, as well as some of their most **popular myths.**

311. **The Incas made beautiful artwork in their textiles,** which were often decorated with images of animals, nature, and the gods.

312. **Inca art was used to decorate the walls of buildings and tell stories about their culture.**

313. Inca history and stories were passed down orally through generations of the same family or group.

314. **The most famous type of Inca stories is creation myths.** They tell about how certain things in their world came to be and what gods were responsible for them.

315. **Many songs and poems from this time told stories about nature, love, war, and religion.**

316. **Inca writers later wrote about the natural world and how people should live in harmony with it,** which is still an important part of their culture today.

317. What literature we do have from the Incas comes from people of Inca descent of later periods. One of **the most famous Inca writers was Wamán Poma de Ayala,** who lived in the 1500s.

318. **Most historians believe that tales about mythical creatures like pumas may have been passed down through generations via quipu storytelling techniques.** The knots on a quipu could be tied in different ways to represent different numbers, so the strings could have been arranged in different patterns to represent different stories.

319. **Geometric motifs, such as bands of repeated triangles, squares, straight and stepped lines,** and stylized plant forms, were commonly painted or etched on Inca pottery.

320. The most famous type of artwork made by the Incas are tapestries woven together using brightly colored threads made from wool or cotton. These tapestries could be hung up on walls like curtains.

321. Animals such as llamas, jaguars, and condors were commonly represented in both stories and art because they held spiritual significance to the Incas.

322. The sun or moon were the most common symbols in Inca art.

323. The most important figure in Inca stories was Viracocha (or Wiraqucha), who was believed to be a powerful god who created the world. He is often represented in paintings and sculptures from this period.

324. One interesting form of storytelling was mnemonic chants that helped people remember important facts and figures without having to write anything down. **These songs are still performed today** in some parts of Peru as part of folkloric traditions honoring ancestors who lived centuries before them.

325. Archaeologists, historians, and linguists have studied quipus for a long time. There is a debate as to whether they are only about statistics, numbers, population, and years or if they perhaps tell a deeper, more intricate story.

326. Even though most artwork from this time has been destroyed or damaged, some pieces remain intact today, like stone walls with carved images or paintings on them.

327. The goldsmiths who worked for the royal families created incredibly detailed sculptures or statuettes out of precious metals, which could be offered up to deities during special ceremonies.

328. The Incas believed in the power of storytelling to teach moral lessons and important values.

329. **Though Inca stories and poems were not written down**, it's likely that elements of them survive among the indigenous peoples of the former Inca Empire, especially in Peru.

330. **One story from this era is called the "Legend of Tunupa,"** which tells the story of an Inca prince who battles with nature gods before finding his true love.

331. **Inca stories often feature characters who must battle the forces of nature or gods to achieve their goals** and demonstrate their courage, strength, and perseverance.

332. **The Incas wove brightly colored feathers** to create intricate patterns and designs.

333. **One of the most famous legends from the Inca Empire is that of Pachacuti,** a great ruler and warrior who conquered many lands and unified them into one kingdom.

334. **Another popular legend tells the story of Manco Capac,** the legendary founder of the Inca civilization who descended from heaven to create a new home for his people in Peru.

335. **The pottery wheel did not exist in the Inca Empire until the arrival of the Spanish,** but Inca ceramists still constructed visually stunning and structurally complex vessels. The clay was pressed against a hardened material to conform to its shape.

Inca Medicine and Health Practices

Examine the world of Inca medicine with this chapter. We'll delve into twenty interesting facts **about their use of herbs, plants, minerals, and spiritual treatments** to heal physical or mental ailments.

336. **The Inca people believed that illnesses were caused by bad spirits.**

337. **Incas used many herbs, plants, and minerals** to make medicine for healing the sick.

338. **Herbs were an important part of Inca medicine.** They could be eaten or used as an ointment.

339. **To diagnose illness, Inca healers would ask questions about symptoms, habits, or dreams** before recommending any treatment.

340. **Herbal teas were commonly used to treat colds, fevers, and other ailments,** while oils derived from plants might be rubbed onto an area for relief from pain.

341. **The Incas believed in the power of natural healing through sun exposure,** which is why they had a practice where individuals would stand out in the open air so sunlight could fall on the exposed parts of their bodies.

342. **Women's fertility was treated using plants like maca root,** which is still used today by Peruvian women hoping to conceive children more easily.

343. **Ancient Inca healers were able to perform operations like trepanation,** which is the drilling of holes in the skull to relieve pressure.

344. **Many remedies incorporated religious rituals,** such as chanting prayers while preparing medicines or herbs to give the medicines more power and potency.

345. **The Inca Empire had a medical system** with professional physicians, surgeons, and herbalists called yachac kamayuks, or "wise people," who treated illnesses and injuries in the community.

346. **The Andean coca plant was considered sacred in ancient times.** Its leaves were chewed before religious ceremonies or long journeys due to its energizing effects, which lasted longer than sugar-based stimulants like coffee.

347. **During healing, some tribes believed that offering an animal soul** would help cure sicknesses afflicting their people.

348. **Inca doctors often used the power of suggestion to treat illnesses,** believing that if a patient was convinced their illness could be cured, it would happen.

349. **Amulets and charms were used as protective talismans against disease or injury,** with each magical item having a specific purpose, such as healing snake bites or protecting a person from lightning strikes.

350. **Herbal baths were popular among affluent Incas** who enjoyed taking long soaks in fragrant oils designed to relax muscles after work or heal injuries sustained during battle.

351. **Ancient Inca physicians knew how air pressure affects a body's chemistry.** They treated altitude sickness caused by traveling between high altitudes over several days with rest at lower elevations.

352. **Syphilis and tuberculosis were two of the most common diseases** in pre-Columbian Inca territories.

353. **The Incas were able to perform blood transfusions!**

354. **After successful operations, patients would often receive gifts like coca leaves** to help reduce pain and promote healing while also offering prayers **to Pachamama (Mother Earth).**

355. **The Inca had a spiritual connection with the environment around them,** believing that all life was connected and could communicate through prayer or sacrifice to help heal ailments afflicting one's body.

Inca Society and Social Structure

Explore twenty fascinating **facts about how Inca society was structured.** Explore how the **Incas saw marriage and what rights women held** during the time of the Inca Empire.

356. **The high priest and the general helped advise the Sapa Inca** and were seen as powerful figures in society.

357. **Inca society was organized into clans,** with each one having its own leader.

358. **There were three main social classes in the** Inca Empire: **the Sapa Inca** and his family, **nobles,** and **commoners.**

359. **The nobles included priests,** most of the professional warriors, and government officials. Almost all of these people had access to wealth and/or power.

360. **Commoners worked in agriculture or the mines or created crafts,** such as weaving textiles for clothing or making pottery for storing food items.

361. **Marriage between people from different social classes was very rare**, although it happened on occasion.

362. **The father headed the Inca family and was responsible for the family's welfare.** If he died, the eldest son or most responsible male took his place.

363. **Women had a comparatively high status in Inca society** for the time and were allowed to own land and property.

364. **The coya, the Inca queen, was often consulted on important political decisions.** She was also responsible for representing the empire at important ceremonies and festivals.

365. **The coya was responsible for overseeing the education of the royal children,** and she was often involved in charitable work.

366. **Every child was expected to learn the Inca language and traditions.**

367. **Nobles were responsible for ruling over their own regions or provinces** within the empire and collecting taxes from those under them on behalf of the Sapa Inca, as well as providing soldiers for his army when needed.

368. **Priests maintained religious temples throughout each region** and performed ceremonies.

369. **Every member of society had duties to perform,** from commoners working on farms to high-ranking officials responsible for governing provinces or even entire empires.

370. **The Incas believed in a strong sense of community.** Everyone had an important role to play in maintaining order and harmony in their society.

371. **Each member of a family worked together on common tasks,** such as farming and building homes, while also having individual responsibilities according to their age and gender.

372. **The homes of officials were nicer and larger than those of commoners.** Their homes were made of stone or adobe, and they had thatched roofs. They were often two or three stories tall, and they had multiple rooms.

373. **The homes of commoners were made of mud bricks**, and they had thatched roofs. They were typically one story tall, and they had only two or three rooms.

374. **Incas females married around sixteen,** while the males married around twenty. The age of marriage depended on social class; nobles tended to marry later than commoners.

375. **Traditional marriage between two people was the rule in the Inca Empire**, but the Sapa Inca was allowed to have more than one wife.

Inca Agriculture and Aquaculture

Uncovering the fascinating field of Inca agriculture and aquaculture. This chapter looks at fifteen interesting facts about how the Inca grew food and watered their crops in the mountainous regions of Peru.

376. **In the fertile highlands of Peru, the Inca grew** corn, potatoes, beans, squash, tomatoes, and more.

377. **Incas also cultivated cotton** for clothing and textiles.

378. **The Incas built terraced fields on steep hillsides** to allow for water drainage so crops could grow better even at higher altitudes.

379. **The Incas had an early form of crop insurance called mit'a,** where farmers could borrow seeds from a government warehouse if their crops failed due to drought or other natural disasters.

380. **Fishing was an important way for them to get food from freshwater sources,** such as rivers, streams, or lakes, and directly off shorelines along the coast where they could find saltwater fish.

381. **The Incas made their fishing nets from a variety of materials,** including cotton, wool, and vegetable fibers.

382. **They had sophisticated aquaculture systems,** where they would farm various types of shellfish, such as mussels, oysters, and clams, in special ponds along with some species of edible seaweeds.

383. **To provide a better habitat for their aquatic animals, the Incas constructed canals** so that water could be brought from other areas into these artificial lakes more easily.

384. **The Incas were one of the first civilizations to start farming llamas,** which provided them with meat and wool for clothing since llama hair is quite warm even when wet.

385. **They also domesticated alpacas, animals like llamas but smaller.** These animals produced an especially soft fiber that was highly prized by royalty at this time due to its fine texture, making it perfect for weaving into beautiful clothing.

386. **One of the most important crops the Incas cultivated was quinoa,** a type of grain native to South America that has become popular today. It contains high amounts of protein, fiber, and minerals.

387. **The Incas were known for using guano** (fertilizer made from bird or bat droppings), which helped increase yields in farming areas by providing essential nutrients, such as nitrogen and phosphorus, to the soil.

388. **The farmers would rotate different fields yearly** so soil fertility wouldn't diminish over time due to continuous planting without breaks in between growing seasons.

389. **The Inca used complex irrigation systems called acequias** (a Spanish word) before the arrival of Europeans. The system is still used today in some areas of Peru and Bolivia.

390. **The Incas had a wide variety of tools for different farming tasks,** such as digging sticks used to plant seeds and long wooden poles with sharp stones attached at the end, which helped break up hard soil so that they could be more easily worked on.

Architecture and Technology

From the majestic Machu Picchu and Sacsayhuamán to other sophisticated engineering feats, this chapter **will unveil the captivating history of Inca architecture and technology.** We'll examine twenty interesting facts about the Incas' incredible building skills.

391. **The Inca built their cities on top of hills** and mountains to protect them from enemies.

392. **They were skilled at building bridges across deep canyons using only ropes, trees, and stones for support.**

393. **Their buildings were made of stone blocks that fit together so precisely** that you couldn't even slide a piece of paper between them.

394. **The Incas had no wheels or beasts of burden like horses or donkeys,** but they still managed to build roads throughout the empire without them.

395. **Machu Picchu is one of the best-known examples of Inca architecture.** It has been designated as a UNESCO World Heritage Site since 1983 due to its incredible engineering, with terraces carved into cliffs and water systems running through it.

396. **The Inca used a technique called ashlar,** an ancient masonry form where stones were cut and shaped to fit together perfectly without mortar or cement.

397. **The Inca used a device called a tupu to hold their stones together** when constructing buildings.

398. **To build tall structures like temples, the Incas would use logs** as scaffolding and then fill in around them with stone blocks for support.

399. **They had no iron or steel tools,** so they used harder rocks like obsidian or bronze-tipped wooden chisels instead.

400. To transport heavy stones, the Incas would roll them on log rollers that were greased with animal fat before placing each block into place. This allowed them to move boulders up to ten tons in weight.

401. The Inca built aqueducts to transport water from the mountains into their cities and agricultural terraces.

402. Inca cities were built with highly advanced engineering techniques, many of which are still being studied today.

403. In Cuzco, they developed an urban plan that divided the city into four sections: Hanan (upper) and **Hurin** (lower) for each side of town, plus two smaller parts called **Camac** and **Chincha** located toward the center of town.

404. Sacsayhuamán was a fortress built on the hill above Cuzco and was made of huge stones, some weighing up to two hundred tons!

405. They created an astronomical observatory site called Chankillo, which consists of thirteen towers aligned along two parallel lines, each facing eastward. It is believed to have been used for measuring seasonal changes or predicting eclipses.

406. The "Zigzag Wall" is a unique feature of Chankillo. It is a long wall that runs along the top of the ridge where the towers are located. The wall zigzags, and it is believed that it was used to track the movement of the sun throughout the year.

407. The Inca used advanced techniques such as corbelling, an arrangement of stones that allowed for a dome-like structure to be made without mortar and with minimal support.

408. The walls of the holy site of Machu Picchu are all aligned with the cardinal directions: north, south, east, and west.

409. They also employed trapezoidal masonry in their buildings, meaning each stone has a slightly different angle to fit with its neighbor. This allowed them to create walls and structures with superior strength than those made from straight-edged blocks.

410. The Incas also used cement made from volcanic ash to bind stones into solid structures, making their buildings last longer than those built without cement.

Inca Warfare and Military Tactics

The Inca Empire would not have been so large if it wasn't for its military. This chapter will reveal twenty intriguing facts about Inca weapons, tactics, and army.

411. **Inca warriors fought with weapons like spears, axes, slingshots, and bows and arrows.**

412. **Warriors had to be very fit and strong to fight in the Inca army.**

413. **The Inca army was composed of two main parts:** professional soldiers called *aucac* and conscripts from the general population known as *yana*.

414. **Among the *aucac* were specialized soldiers,** including those responsible for gathering intelligence on enemies before the battle began.

415. **The soldiers wore protective armor made of leather, cloth, or animal skins** that they decorated with feathers and paint to look fierce in battle.

416. **Soldiers would form lines or columns while fighting so they could use their shields to protect themselves against incoming arrows or rocks** thrown by the enemy.

417. **The commanders usually stayed at home bases where they could communicate orders more efficiently through drums, whistles, and banners** instead of relying on verbal commands alone, as most armies did back then.

418. **When the Incas wanted to show their strength, they would march through enemy territories with large groups of warriors carrying shields and weapons** as an intimidating show of force.

419. **The estolica, or spear thrower, is a tool that uses the force of leverage to increase the velocity of a thrown spear.** The Inca used them, as did the Aztecs of Mexico, who called them atlatl.

420. **The Inca commanders, known as capac apus or "war chiefs," would gather intelligence about their enemies** and study their tactics and defenses. They would then develop strategies that played to **the strengths of the Inca military,** such as their discipline, numerical advantage, and knowledge of the terrain.

421. **The military was divided into two main divisions:** infantry soldiers equipped with spears and slingshots and a small number of soldiers armed with bows, arrows, and spears.

422. **A unique form of award existed during this period:** small gold llama figures were rewarded for successful military campaigns or loyalty to the Sapa Inca.

423. **The Incas used rituals to prepare for battle** and might have included events like painting stones with images of snakes or birds and sacrificing a black llama to represent the enemy's weakness.

424. **Inca commanders usually positioned archers at the top of hills** so that they could shoot arrows down on enemies below them from a safer distance.

425. **The Incas had no cavalry.** Llamas were used to carry supplies during wars but did not serve as mounts for soldiers.

426. Inca leaders were known for their bravery and willingness to fight until the death if necessary, providing an example for other soldiers to follow when engaging in battle.

427. **Before the battle began, priests would bless the soldiers** so they felt safe and secure when fighting against enemy forces.

428. **Women also played an important role in the military by working as healers** or taking care of wounded troops after fights were over.

429. **Warrior training generally began in childhood** in the form of ritual fights and martial arts training.

430. **Men who served in the Inca army were between twenty-five and fifty years old.**

Education in the Inca Empire

This chapter will unveil ten facts about the Inca Empire's education system. Learn what students commonly learned about and how children were taught lessons.

431. **The Incas had a system of separation between noble and common education.**

432. **The education system of nobles in Inca society consisted of a four-year program** with defined terms of courses. In the first year, **students learned the Quechua language.** In the second year, **students studied religion.** In their third year, **they started to be taught quipu.** In their fourth year, **they focused on religion again.**

433. **The amautas taught children,** especially those in the noble class.

434. **The Inca education system was based on memorization,** with students being required to memorize long poems, songs, and stories.

435. **Yachaywasi is a Quechua term that translates to "house of knowledge" or "house of learning."** It was where they sent children of noble families to receive an education.

436. **Astronomy played a big part in education.** Incas believed understanding the stars could help them predict weather patterns and plan agricultural activities accordingly.

437. **Formal education was not available to children of peasants or craftspeople, so they learned from their parents.**

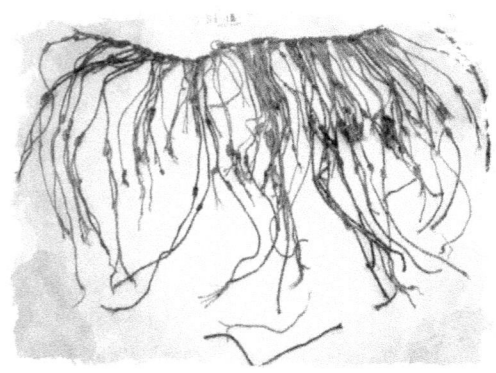

438. **Commoners learned practical skills such as farming techniques** to help support their families as they grew older.

439. **Girls were chosen from the villages and given training in spinning, weaving, cooking,** chicha-making, and religion.

440. **To achieve full status within the Inca nobility, students had to pass difficult examinations.**

Language of the Incas

This chapter will discuss the language of the Incas, one of the oldest languages in South America. We'll dive into **fifteen interesting facts about Quechua,** its various dialects, and how the Spanish impacted the language.

441. **Quechua is also called Runasimi, which means "people's language."** It was the Inca people's spoken language.

442. **Quechua is an agglutinate language, meaning it includes words made up of morphemes** (prefixes or suffixes) that can be combined in various ways to create new meanings for words. This makes Quechua very expressive.

443. **Quechua has two main dialects. Runa Simi** was the dialect spoken by the Incas and their subjects in the central highlands of Peru. It is the ancestor of the modern **Quechua I dialect.**

444. **Qulla** Simi **was the dialect spoken by the Incas** and their subjects in the northern and southern highlands of Peru, as well as in Ecuador, Bolivia, Chile, and Argentina. **It is the ancestor of the modern Quechua II dialect.**

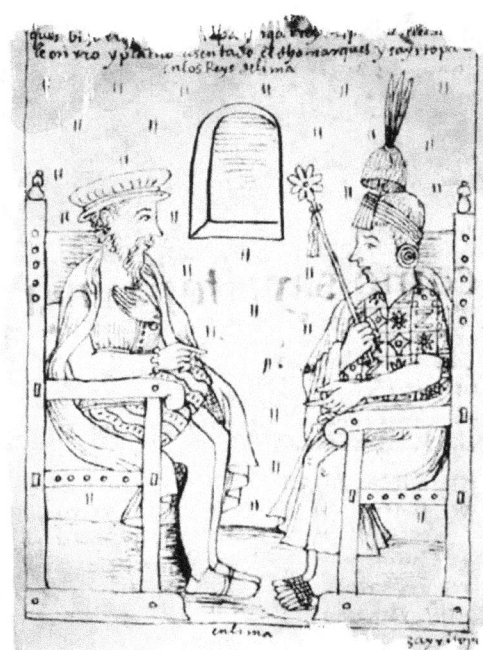

445. **For a long time, linguists believed that Quechua was a noun-based language.** While it is true that Quechua has a large number of nouns, it also has a large number of verbs. In fact, some linguists have argued that **Quechua is actually a verb-oriented language.**

446. **Quechua has a variety of slang terms that are used in everyday speech,** as well as more formal words reserved for official documents and religious ceremonies.

447. **Quechua is far older than the Incas** and possibly originated more than a thousand years before their time.

448. **Quechua is a tonal language,** so the same word spoken in different tones can have very different meanings.

449. **Quechua is an indigenous language of Peru, Bolivia, Ecuador, Argentina, and Chile** (though it is spoken to a lesser degree in those places).

450. **It is believed that Quechua had no written form until Spanish colonizers** introduced it in the 16th century CE.

451. **The language has been strongly influenced by other cultures** like the Aymara, Huarpe, and Mapuche peoples, who all lived alongside each other in South America at one point or another in history.

452. **Quechua was recognized by UNESCO as an official living cultural heritage of humanity in 2003.** This means that UNESCO recognizes Quechua as a living language that is important to the cultural heritage of the Andes region.

453. **There are many "Neo-Quechuan" dialects spoken today** that are a mix of Spanish and Quechua.

454. **Inca leaders were known for their eloquence when speaking and would often use metaphors, similes, and poetic language** to inspire people or make a point.

455. **Today, the traditional dress of the Andean people is often embroidered with Quechuan words or phrases.** This way, they can show their culture without having to say anything.

Record-keeping System of the Incas

This chapter will take a closer look at the remarkable record-keeping system of the Incas. Delve into ten interesting facts about quipu and how it was used.

456. **The Incas created a system of record-keeping called quipu** despite not having a written alphabet.

457. **Quipu means "knot" in Quechua.** It is now recognized as a symbol of tradition, and it's occasionally used as religious material in their communal celebrations.

458. **The quipu was a complex knot-tying system used by the ancient Inca civilization to record information,** ranging from census data and tax records to historical events and religious ceremonies.

459. **Quipu or khipu has an intricate design.** The use of different colored strings makes it a fascinating and unique method of record-keeping in the ancient world.

460. **The different colors on a quipu** (pronounced *kipu*) **represented different concepts** or ideas. The specific meanings of the colors varied depending on the region and the purpose of the quipu.

461. It may surprise you that the **Incas did not develop the quipu. The quipu was first discovered in Wari, a Middle Horizon** (an earlier South American period) society. The Incas later adopted the quipu system for administrative purposes.

462. **About a hundred years ago, the decimal system indicated by the knots on quipus was deciphered.**

463. **The largest quipus have as many as 1,500 threads,** which may be knotted in many ways that symbolize different meanings.

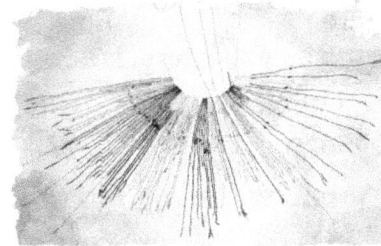

464. **The quipus were kept and maintained by readers known as quipucamayocs or khipukamayuqs.** Additionally, there were even some shamans who were taught the complexity of the knot system.

465. **Most quipus have a thick, horizontal main cord from which some thinner pendant cords hang,** anywhere from one to over a thousand. Thus, many pendant cords have knots on them, which usually stand for numbers in a system called base ten.

Trade and Economy of the Incas

This chapter delves into the intricacies of Inca trade and the empire's economy. These fifteen facts cover information about **the bartering system, government policies, and taxes.** While taxes may not be anyone's idea of a fun time, these facts will be fun to whip out at dinnertime!

466. **The Incas didn't use money and didn't need it either.** Their economy and political system were set up so well that everyone could meet their basic needs.

467. **People traded for things they needed** using the barter system.

468. **Each Inca family had to give one-seventh of their harvest each year** to the government. In return, they would get food, clothing, and other necessary items from a central storehouse.

469. **The ayllu was essential to the Inca Empire's economic growth.** Ayllus were families living in the same community and were the core of the economic productivity of the empire, specializing in producing goods or crops depending on their location.

470. **The Incas collected taxes from different regions in exchange for protection from their military forces** and access to goods produced by other parts of the empire.

471. **Collective labor was evident in the Inca economy.** Ayni was the idea that people in the community should assist each other.

472. **People would engage in** *mink'a***, voluntary labor to help improve a community.** This could be building new aqueducts or helping to raise a new home.

473. **Each family cultivated their property but did not own it;** the Inca government owned it.

474. **The ayllu utilized the area to grow food for the family's livelihood.**

475. The Inca Empire's central resources were agricultural land and labor, mines, and fresh water.

476. Nobles and other significant Incas were exempted from paying labor taxes. Even when nobles died, they could still hold property, and their relatives or estate managers might continue to accrue money on their behalf. **This system of inheritance helped to ensure** that the wealth and power of the elite remained within their families.

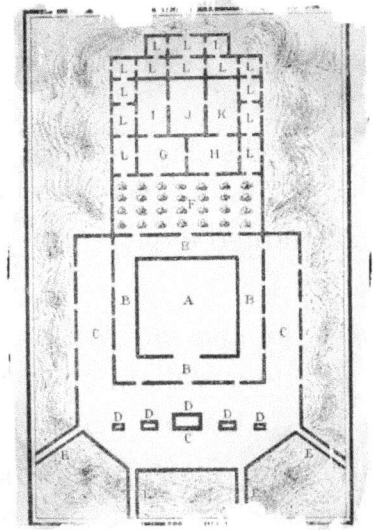

477. Colcas, or government-controlled storage facilities, housed food, merchandise, and raw materials to protect against uncertain harvests or political turmoil.

478. The Incas traded with neighboring cultures, some of whom they took over in later years.

479. One of them was the Chachapoya, who lived in the Amazon rainforest. They were known for their elaborate fortifications and their skilled warriors. **The Incas traded with the Chachapoya** for gold, silver, and other metals.

480. The Incas had sea-worthy boats that voyaged up and down the coast of western South America to trade and fish.

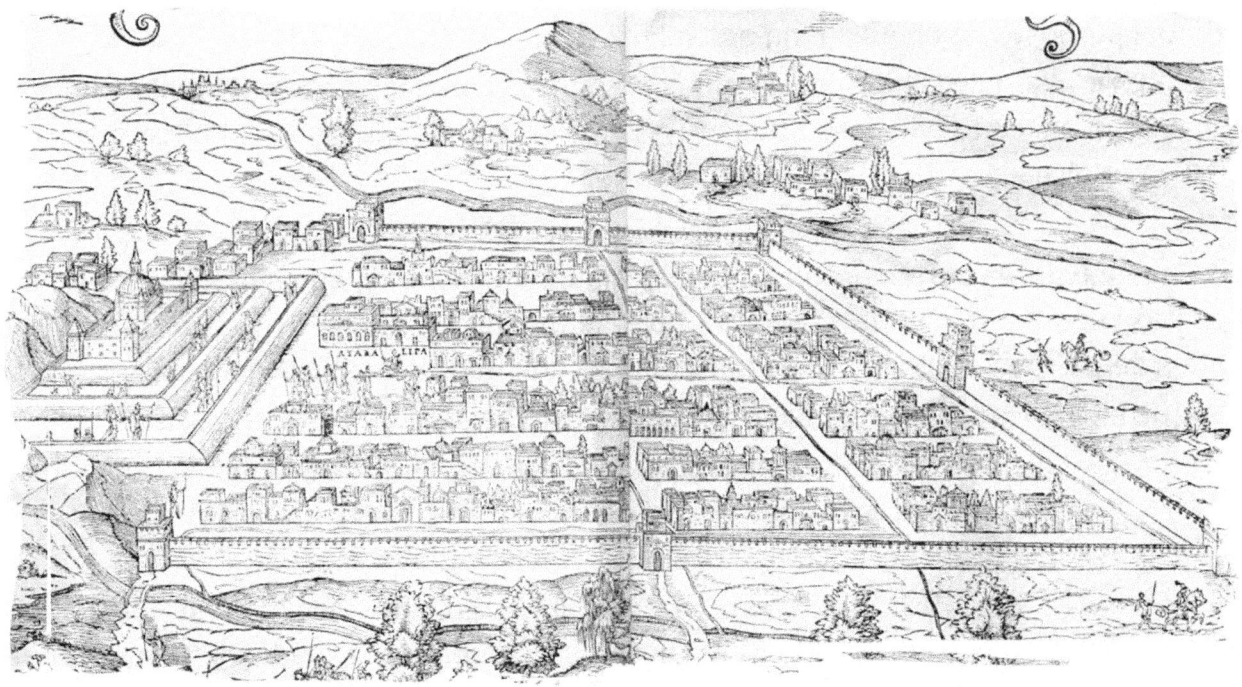

Inca Music

Learn the captivating history of Inca music in this chapter. Discover ten interesting facts about how music was used, common instruments, and how Inca music is still celebrated today.

481. **Almost all Inca musical instruments were based on traditions** that began about four thousand years ago in the Andean Highlands.

482. **The Incas used music to tell stories, express emotions, and pass down knowledge from one generation to the next through songs.**

483. **The Incas had a complex system of musical notation** that was used to record and transmit music. This system was based on a series of symbols that represented different pitches and rhythms.

484. **Inca music often featured themes related to nature,** such as birdsongs, waterfalls, and rainbows.

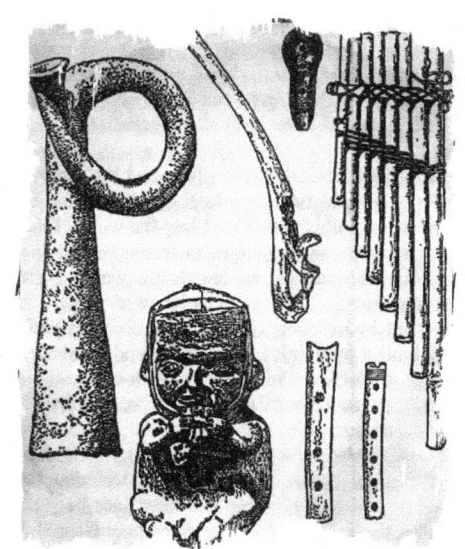

485. **Inca music served social functions,** such as entertainment at festivals, but also spiritual purposes, such as during sacred rites.

486. **Incas also used their voices alone without accompanying instruments.** Singing notes in an ancient style called huayno is still popular among Andean cultures across Peru and Bolivia.

487. **Inca music was often accompanied by clapping, chanting, and singing.** This rhythm helped to keep the music moving and to create a sense of excitement. It also helped to create a sense of community, as people clapped, chanted, and sang together.

488. **The Incas used music to talk to the dead, heal the sick, and bury the dead.**

489. **The drum (*huancar*) was made with a hollowed-out timber base and dried llama skin stretched firmly around it.** Drums were made in a range of sizes to make various sounds.

490. **The *antara*, or panpipe, was the Incas' most unique and artistically built musical instrument.** It was made up of seven flutes that were grouped in descending sequence. The musician would blow over the opening, with each flute making a unique sound.

Inca Jewelry

This section will unveil the development of Inca jewelry in Peru from the 18ᵗʰ century to the present. Let's examine ten fascinating facts about the evolution of jewelry-making techniques and the cultural significance of Inca jewelry.

491. **Jewelry-making techniques evolved over time.** For example, when Spanish colonists arrived, they introduced **new materials like glass beads and metals like copper, which allowed more intricate designs to be created using filigree work** or the granulation method (an advanced technique involving tiny metal balls joined together without solder on top of plate cutouts to form patterns like spirals or circles).

492. **In colonial times, it was common for wealthy families to commission custom-made pieces from European jewelers,** but local artisans also continued to craft their own unique pieces.

493. **Inca jewelry was used as a symbol of wealth and status.** The wealthiest families would wear large gold necklaces with intricate designs and stones set in them as a sign of their power or rank within society.

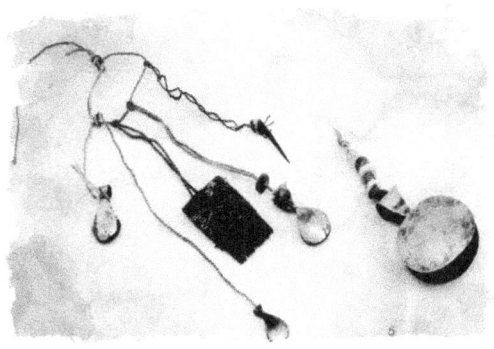

494. **In colonial times, it became popular to use silver instead of gold** because it was easier to obtain and less expensive, allowing more people access to beautiful jewelry.

495. **The most common shapes were discs, circles, crescents, or spirals,** which represented cycles, such as moon phases or seasons. These symbols still appear today in Peruvian designs today.

496. By the 19ᵗʰ century, **different materials began being introduced into traditional Inca jewelry,** like coral beads from Mediterranean countries.

497. **Today's Inca jewelry is characterized by its vibrant colors** derived from natural gemstones found all over Peru, such as turquoise and lapis lazuli.

498. **Traditional designs have been preserved,** but new techniques, such as laser engraving, are being used to create more intricate patterns in pieces that represent cultural heritage.

499. **Jewelry has become an important part of the Peruvian identity,** with many artisans dedicating their lives to creating beautiful pieces for not only themselves but also people worldwide.

500. **Traditional Inca jewelry often features symbols like pumas** (representing strength) or condors (representing freedom).

Sources and Additional References

Lane, Kevin. *The Inca: Lost Civilizations*. 2022.

MacQuarrie, Kim. *The Last Days of the Incas*. 2008.

Malpass, Michael. *Daily Life in the Inca Empire*. 2009.

Sullivan, William. *The Secret of the Incas: Myth, Astronomy, and the War Against Time*. 1997.

Wellman, Billy. *The Inca Empire: An Enthralling Overview of the Incas*. 2023.

Check out another book in the series

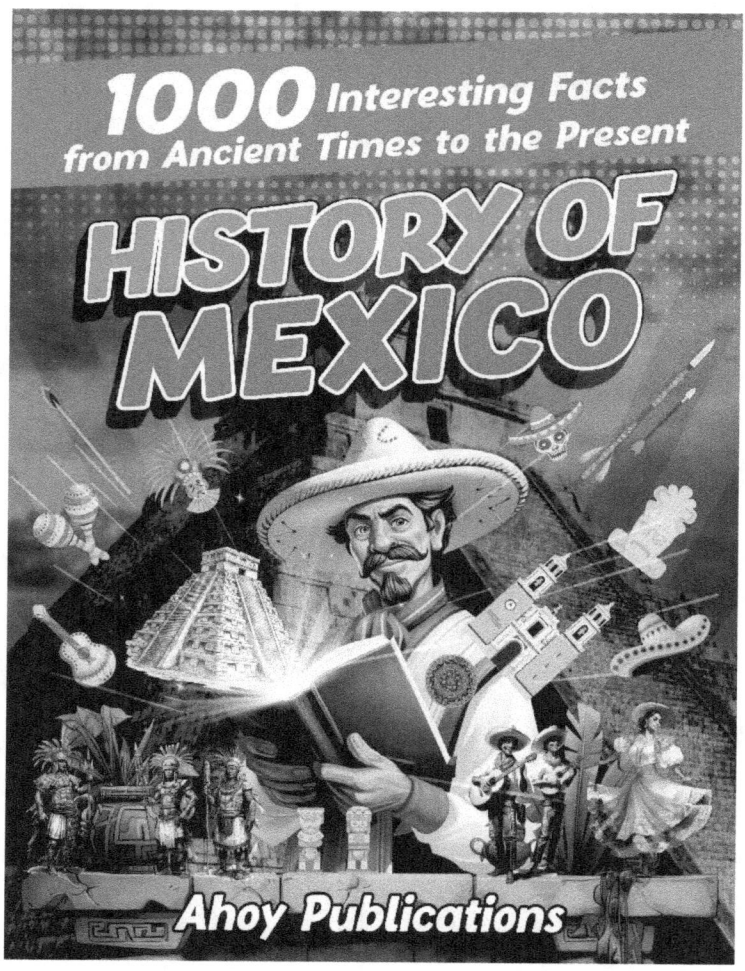